MW01204182

WORLD OF
MUSHROOMS

The mission of Storey Publishing is to serve our customers by publishing practical information that encourages personal independence in harmony with the environment.

Text by Pauline Payen
Translated by Celyn Harding-Jones
Illustrations by Zelda Pressigout
Design of this translated edition by HK Goldstein

First published in France under the title: *Champignons*

© éditions Panthera, 2023

English language translation rights arranged through Ttipi agency, France.

The information in this book is provided only as a resource. Any reader who forages for wild mushrooms and chooses to ingest them does so at his or her own risk; without a 100 percent positive identification, no wild mushroom should ever be consumed. Consulting with an expert mushroom forager, who can identify the mushrooms in person, is recommended.

All rights reserved. Hachette Book Group supports the right to free expression and the value of copyright. The purpose of copyright is to encourage writers and artists to produce the creative works that enrich our culture. The scanning, uploading, and distribution of this book without permission is a theft of the author's intellectual property. If you would like permission to use material from the book (other than for review purposes), please contact permissions@hbgusa.com. Thank you for your support of the author's rights.

The information in this book is true and complete to the best of our knowledge. All recommendations are made without guarantee on the part of the author or Storey Publishing. The author and publisher disclaim any liability in connection with the use of this information.

The publisher is not responsible for websites (or their content) that are not owned by the publisher.

Storey books may be purchased in bulk for business, educational, or promotional use. Special editions or book excerpts can also be created to specification. For details, please contact your local bookseller or the Hachette Book Group Special Markets Department at special.markets@hbgusa.com.

Storey Publishing
210 MASS MoCA Way
North Adams, MA 01247
storey.com

Storey Publishing is an imprint of Workman Publishing, a division of Hachette Book Group, Inc., 1290 Avenue of the Americas, New York, NY 10104. The Storey Publishing name and logo are registered trademarks of Hachette Book Group, Inc.

Distributed in Europe by Hachette Livre, 58 rue Jean Bleuzen, 92 178 Vanves Cedex, France
Distributed in the United Kingdom by Hachette Book Group, UK, Carmelite House, 50 Victoria Embankment, London EC4Y 0DZ

ISBNs: 978-1-63586-929-3 (hardcover); 978-1-63586-930-9 (ebook)

Printed in Humen Town, Dongguan, China by R. R. Donnelley on paper from responsible sources
10 9 8 7 6 5 4 3 2 1

APS

Library of Congress Cataloging-in-Publication Data on file

WORLD OF MUSHROOMS

Pauline Payen

ILLUSTRATIONS BY **Zelda Pressigout**

Storey Publishing

You'll find many plants and animals living in the forest, but that's not all . . .
Can you guess who else lives here?

Mushrooms! No doubt you've seen them before.
But how well do you really know them?

Mushrooms are alive, just like a daisy is, or a dog, or you!
But mushrooms are neither plants nor animals.

In the undergrowth of the forest, mushrooms are everywhere! At first they might look similar, but there are many kinds of mushrooms, and they grow in many different ways.

All mushrooms are fungi, but not all fungi are mushrooms—a mushroom typically has a **stem** and a **cap**.

Some mushrooms are known as **saprophytes**, which means they feed on the remains of dead plants (like old leaves or bark) or animals. Saprophytes may even feed on animal droppings!

Yummy! A dead tree!

Some mushrooms live in harmony with trees. They are **symbiotic**. That means that the mushroom and tree help each other survive.

Lichen is formed by fungi that live symbiotically with **algae**, which make food from sunlight, like plants.

I like this tree the best!

Parasitic mushrooms feed off of living plants. Once a plant is attacked, it often ends up dying.

Next, let's learn the different parts of a mushroom!

Have you ever observed a mushroom up close? Let's take a look at the parasol mushroom.

This part on top is called the cap, or the **pileus**. It's protected by a very thin skin called the **cuticle**.

The cap is held up by what looks like a thick stem—the **stipe**.

The small tube around the stem is called a **ring**.

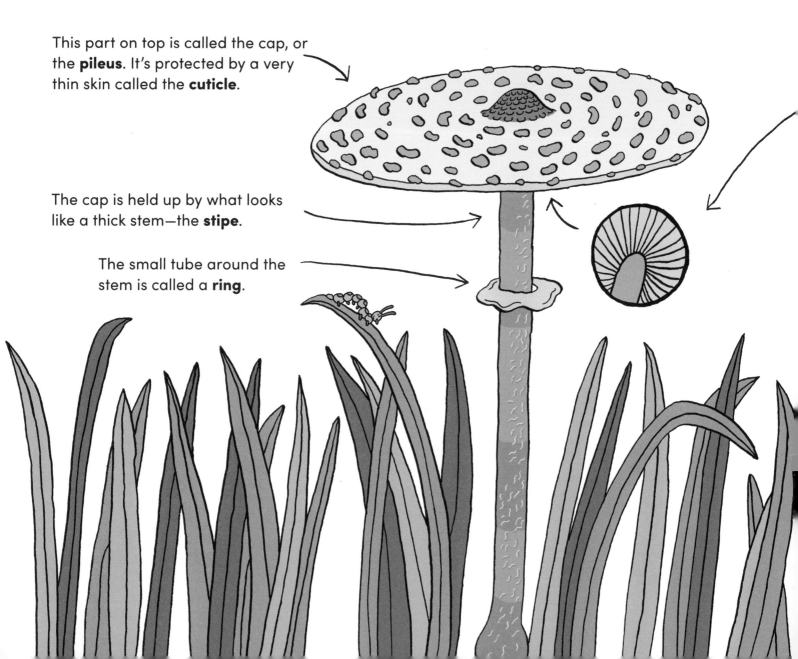

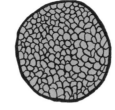  

The part on the underside of the cap is called the **hymenium**. The hymenium of the parasol mushroom has folds in the shape of knife blades. These folds are called the **lamellae**, or gills.

Each mushroom has a unique cap!

And different caps have different kinds of hymenia. Some have small tubes with holes at the ends. Others have small prickly spikes. And still others have gills (like the parasol mushroom) or folds.

Invisible Fungi

You can see some fungi, like the parasol mushroom, easily with the naked eye. But others are so tiny that you can only see them with a microscope! These microscopic fungi hide in plain sight—in the air, on decaying trees and leaves, and even on your skin!

This is another parasol mushroom. Its cap is not yet open, so we call it a **drumstick**.

But what you see here is only a very small part of the mushroom . . .

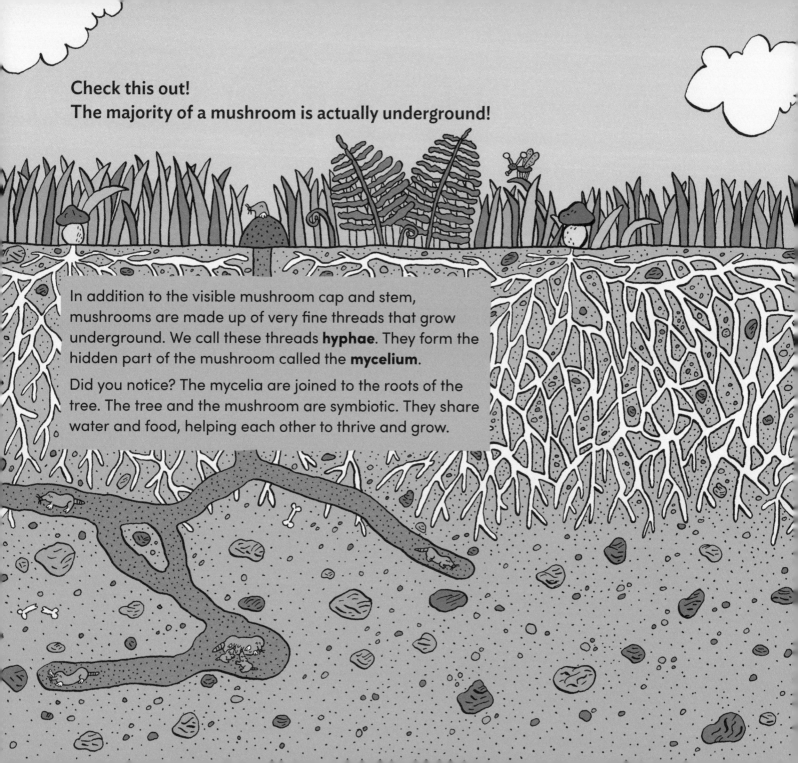

Check this out!
The majority of a mushroom is actually underground!

In addition to the visible mushroom cap and stem, mushrooms are made up of very fine threads that grow underground. We call these threads **hyphae**. They form the hidden part of the mushroom called the **mycelium**.

Did you notice? The mycelia are joined to the roots of the tree. The tree and the mushroom are symbiotic. They share water and food, helping each other to thrive and grow.

Scientists call the part of the mushroom that is aboveground—the part that we can see—the **sporophore**. The sporophore is the part that we usually think of as a mushroom—but it's only part of it!

Living with Trees

The hoof fungus grows on trees, not on the ground. Its mycelia extend inside the tree trunk, where it feeds on the wood.

The sporophore helps the mushroom to reproduce. Here's how.

2

The spores are spread by wind. Each spore begins to grow threads, called hyphae, in a process called **germination**.

1

When the mushroom is fully mature, the underside of the cap—the hymenium—opens. It releases dust made up of light, tiny **spores.** Spores are to mushrooms what seeds are to plants.

TA-DAH! THE CYCLE STARTS ALL OVER AGAIN . . .

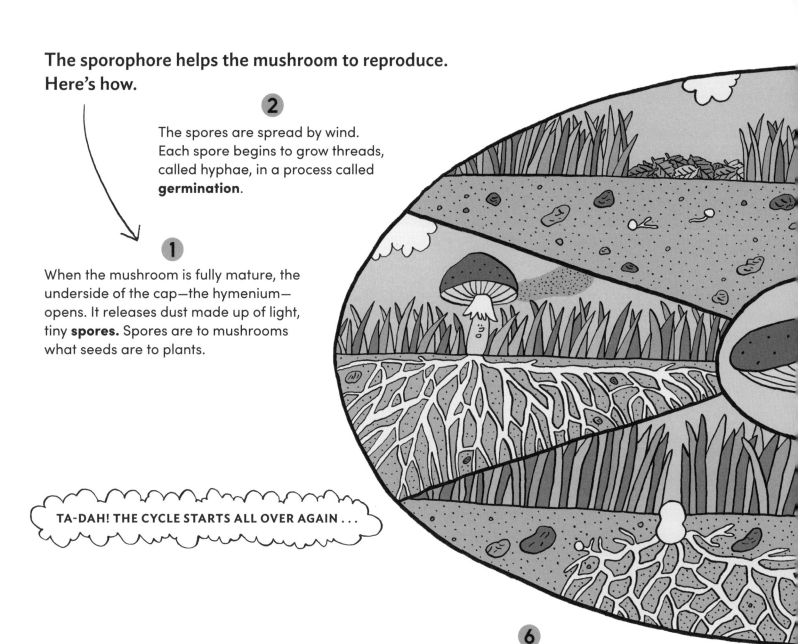

6

As the primordium grows bigger, it emerges from the ground and will continue to grow until it becomes a full-size mushroom.

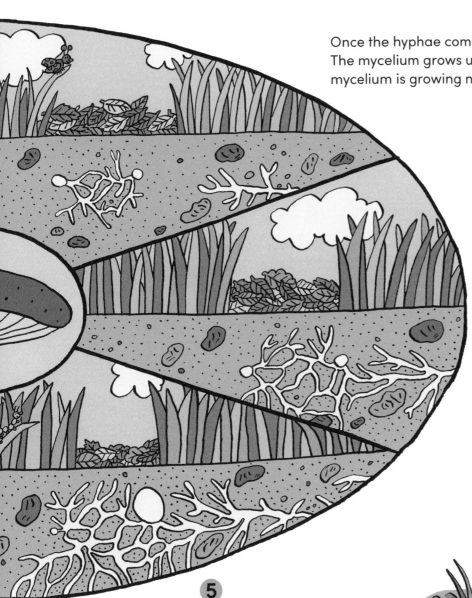

3

Once the hyphae come together, they form a mycelium. The mycelium grows underground. Oh, look! Another mycelium is growing nearby.

4

The two mycelia grow toward each other and join up. What's going to happen next?

Spore Explosion

It's rare to see most kinds of mushrooms release their spores. But certain mushrooms, like the puffball, release their spores if you press them. Poof! A big cloud of spores comes out and gets blown away by the wind.

5

Once connected, the two mycelia create what looks like a ball that will grow underground. This is called the **primordium**.

In nature, mushrooms aren't just there to look pretty. They're actually important parts of ecosystems!

Undergrowth Scavengers

By feeding on the remains of dead animals and plants, mushrooms help keep the soil clean. They are nature's garbage collectors and recyclers, and they turn what they eat into soil that helps plants grow!

At the Table

Like plants, mushrooms also serve as food for many animals, including us humans! Mushrooms play an important role in the food chain.

Give and Take

The underground parts of mushrooms, the mycelia, can join with the roots of plants. This allows plants and mushrooms to exchange resources and help each other! The mushroom provides the plant with much-needed water and **mineral salts**, which it draws from the soil. In exchange, the plant gives the mushroom some of the sugars it makes. Clever, right?

Forest Communicators

Even more incredibly, by mingling their mycelia with the roots of trees, mushrooms form a connection that allows the trees to communicate. For example, if an animal comes to graze on the leaves of a tree, the tree being attacked sends a signal through its branches, to its trunk, and down to its roots. The warning signal passes through the mycelium of the mushroom until it reaches the roots of another tree. The tree that receives the alert makes chemicals that make its own leaves toxic or bad tasting, and the animal then stops grazing. A very effective defense system—all thanks to mushrooms!

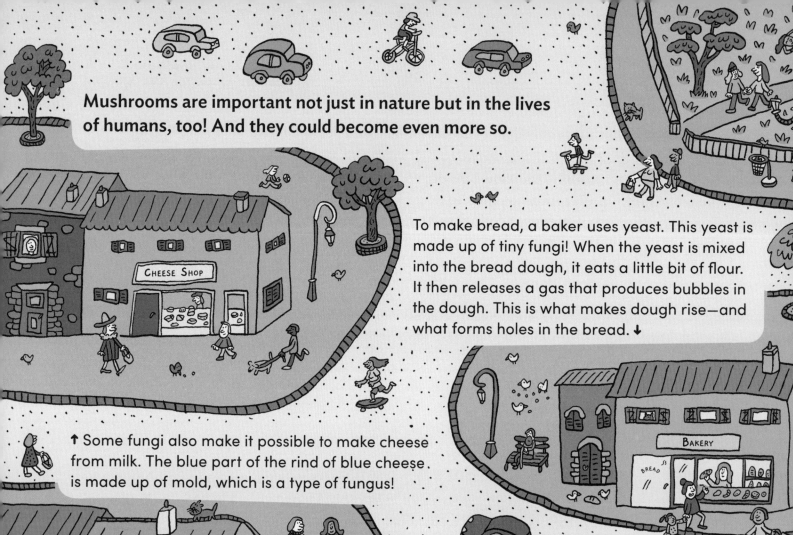

Mushrooms are important not just in nature but in the lives of humans, too! And they could become even more so.

To make bread, a baker uses yeast. This yeast is made up of tiny fungi! When the yeast is mixed into the bread dough, it eats a little bit of flour. It then releases a gas that produces bubbles in the dough. This is what makes dough rise—and what forms holes in the bread. ↓

↑ Some fungi also make it possible to make cheese from milk. The blue part of the rind of blue cheese is made up of mold, which is a type of fungus!

← A fungus called penicillium is used to make **penicillin**, a drug that kills germs.

Scientists are researching how to use mushrooms to make fuel. ↓

Mushrooms don't just grow in the wild but can be cultivated on mushroom farms. These farms are often underground, in dark, cold, damp places, because that is where mushrooms thrive.

Other researchers are studying a mushroom that can break down plastic. This could be a great idea for cleaning up plastic waste!

Mushrooms help plants grow in farmers' fields, just like they do in nature. →

Mushrooms live all over the world—sometimes in surprising places!

Mycelium XXL

The largest living thing in the world known today is . . . a mushroom! The mycelia of the *Armillaria ostoyae* extend in the soil in eastern Oregon over an area as large as 1,500 football fields. And the mycelia weigh as much as three blue whales!

Luminous!

Did you know that there are several types of mushrooms around the world that produce ligh They are said to be **bioluminescent**.

Precious Mushrooms

The most expensive mushroom is the truffle! Truffles grow in the ground and have a very special smell. Humans train dogs and pigs to find them. Truffles can be found in many countries—France, Italy, and Spain are especially well known for them.

On Every Plate

The button mushroom is the most commonly eaten mushroom in the world. It is mainly cultivated in the Netherlands, Poland, and China.

Thriving Together

In Central America, leafcutter ants cultivate *Lepiotaceae* fungus in their nests for food. They cut and grind leaves to feed to it. The mushroom grows and in turn is eaten by the ants!

What Goes Around

Sometimes mushrooms grow next to each other and form circles, which are nicknamed **fairy rings**. This strange phenomenon occurs around the world.

Now that you've gotten to know mushrooms, go outside and have fun observing them in the wild!

ALL ABOUT MUSHROOM FORAGING

Some people go **foraging** for mushrooms, which means they search for and harvest ones in the wild that are good to eat.

Note: Only knowledgeable foragers should eat mushrooms they find in the wild, because many of them are poisonous.

Where and When?

Mushrooms like warm temperatures and humidity. The best time to pick them is in the spring or fall, when it rains a lot, though it depends on the mushroom species! Many mushrooms grow in the forest because dead trees and leaves provide plentiful food sources. They also grow in meadows or marshy areas.

Responsible Foraging

Foragers must pay attention to their surroundings, being careful not to damage nearby plants or disturb the dead leaves that cover the ground. They should also avoid moving rocks or dead wood. If they have to move something, they should put everything back in its place! The golden rule of foraging is to not pick too many mushrooms at once and to leave immature mushrooms where they are. Also, foragers should always ask permission before foraging on private land and be sure they know the rules before picking mushrooms on public land.

Careful Harvesting

Harvesting mushrooms requires using a knife to carefully clear the area around the stem before gently removing the mushroom from the ground by hand. Foragers must have a healthy respect for all mushrooms, because many are poisonous!

Caution!

Mushroom foragers only pick and eat mushrooms they are completely sure are safe to eat. While some mushrooms are good to eat, many others contain poison and can be dangerous for humans. People who want to forage but don't know mushrooms well should go with an experienced guide.

Any mushrooms a guide assures you are safe to eat must be cooked first.

Foraging Equipment

A small mirror to examine under the cap

A small knife

Walking shoes or boots

A mushroom guidebook

A magnifying glass to observe details

A basket

A stick to push aside plants and dead leaves

Mushrooms come in all colors, shapes, and sizes. Here are a few common ones you might find.

CHANTERELLE

The chanterelle grows in woods and forests. It is also known as the girolle.

STICKY BUN

This mushroom grows in forests, but only under pine trees. It is also called a slippery jack.

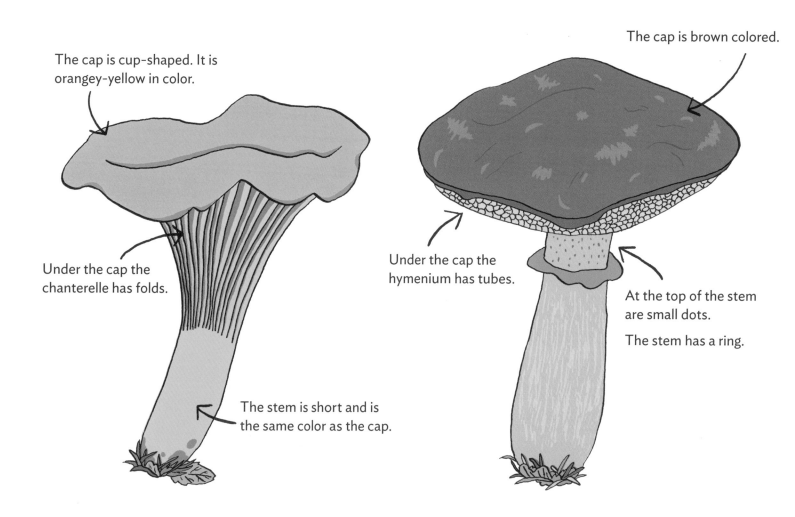

The cap is cup-shaped. It is orangey-yellow in color.

Under the cap the chanterelle has folds.

The stem is short and is the same color as the cap.

The cap is brown colored.

Under the cap the hymenium has tubes.

At the top of the stem are small dots.

The stem has a ring.

I love mushrooms!

BLACK TRUMPET

This mushroom grows in woods and forests. It often grows in clusters.

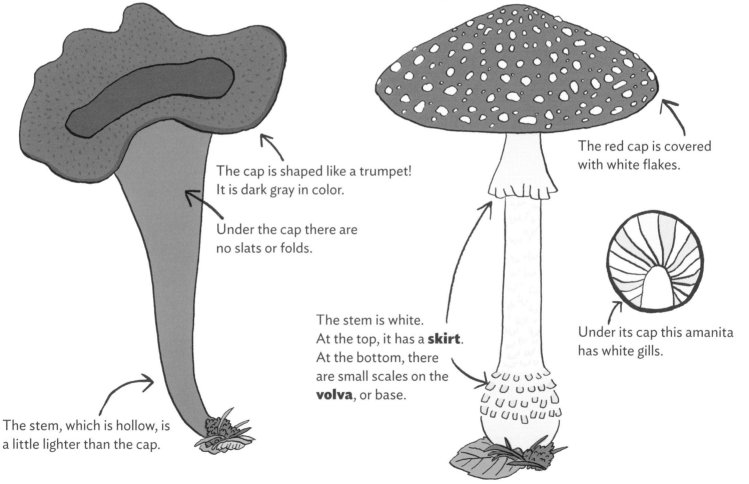

The cap is shaped like a trumpet! It is dark gray in color.

Under the cap there are no slats or folds.

The stem, which is hollow, is a little lighter than the cap.

FLY AMANITA

Watch out, this mushroom is poisonous! It grows in woods and forests. We call it a fly killer because in the past humans used it to repel insects.

The red cap is covered with white flakes.

The stem is white. At the top, it has a **skirt**. At the bottom, there are small scales on the **volva**, or base.

Under its cap this amanita has white gills.

DEATH CAP

Watch out, this mushroom is poisonous!
It grows in woods and forests.

PORCINI MUSHROOM

This mushroom grows in woods and forests and is highly sought after by mushroom pickers.

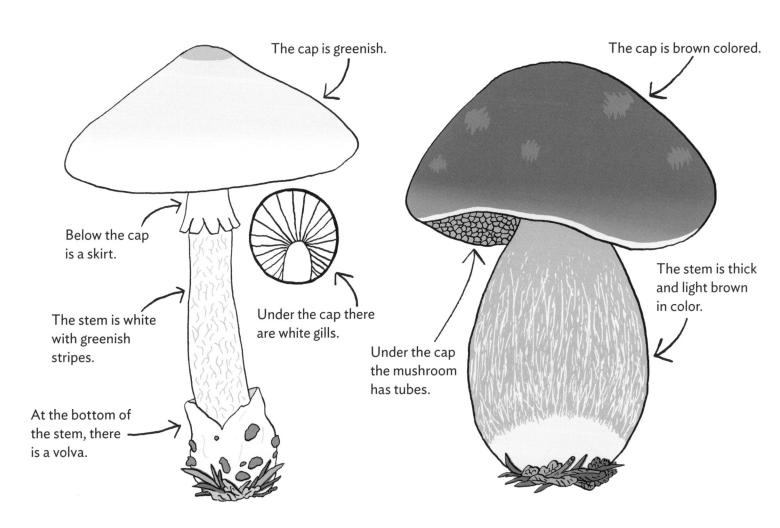

The cap is greenish.

Below the cap is a skirt.

The stem is white with greenish stripes.

Under the cap there are white gills.

At the bottom of the stem, there is a volva.

The cap is brown colored.

The stem is thick and light brown in color.

Under the cap the mushroom has tubes.

PUFFBALL

Watch out, this mushroom has some toxic lookalikes. **This mushroom grows in woods and forests and sometimes "farts"—it expels its spores in clouds of "smoke" and gives off a bad smell.**

SATAN'S BOLETE

Watch out, this mushroom is poisonous! **It grows in woods and forests and is named after the devil because it is red in color.**

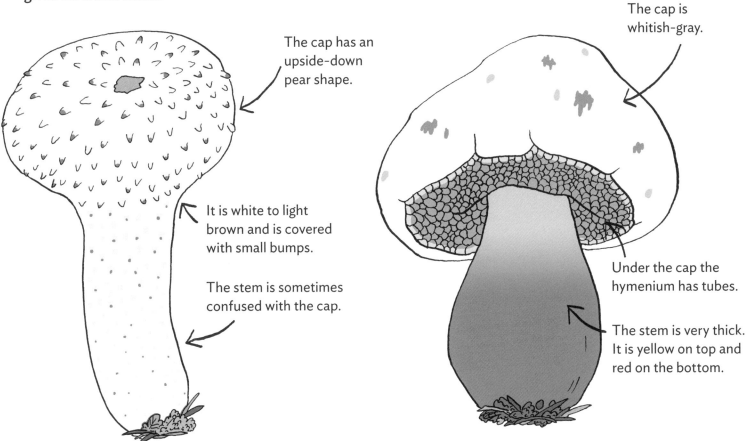

The cap has an upside-down pear shape.

It is white to light brown and is covered with small bumps.

The stem is sometimes confused with the cap.

The cap is whitish-gray.

Under the cap the hymenium has tubes.

The stem is very thick. It is yellow on top and red on the bottom.

SWEET TOOTH

This mushroom grows in woods and forests. It is one of the only mushrooms that can still be found growing after the first frost!

This mushroom has a funny, bumpy cap.

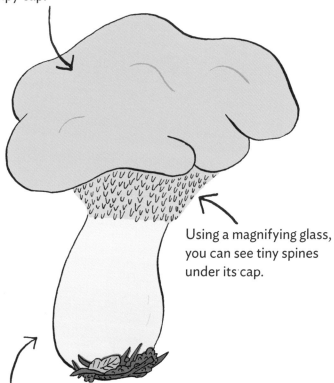

Using a magnifying glass, you can see tiny spines under its cap.

The stem of the sweet tooth is creamy white in color.

YELLOW MOREL

This mushroom grows in woods and forests. It is unusual in that it grows in the springtime.

The cap is light brown in color and looks like a sponge.

This mushroom is hollow inside. Cut it in half from top to bottom to see!

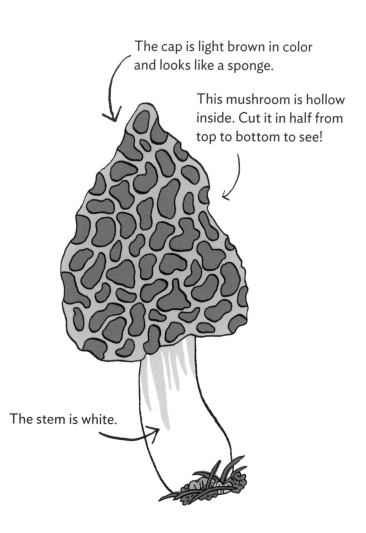

The stem is white.

BEEFSTEAK FUNGUS

This mushroom grows on tree trunks and stumps. It is also called an ox tongue mushroom.

The cap is shaped like a tongue! It is dark red in color.

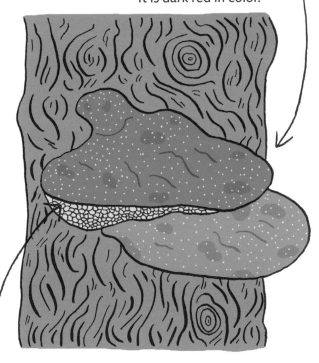

Under the cap the beefsteak fungus has tubes. You can only see them with a magnifying glass.

OYSTER MUSHROOM

This mushroom grows on tree trunks and stumps. It is one of the few known carnivorous mushrooms.

The oyster mushroom has several caps, one above the other. Together, they have the shape and color of an oyster shell!

Under its cap the oyster mushroom has white gills.

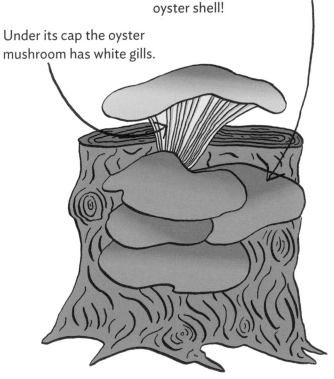

ORANGE PEEL FUNGUS

This mushroom grows in sandy soils. Its hymenium is located inside the cup.

This mushroom's curving cup shape resembles an orange peel.

It is easily spotted thanks to its bright orange color, which is lighter on the outside.

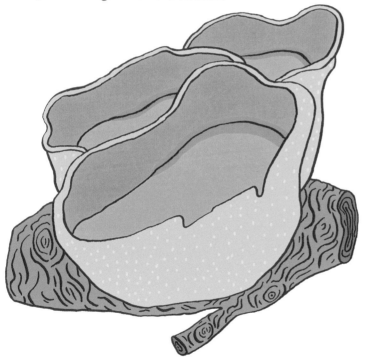

HOOF FUNGUS

This mushroom cannot be eaten but is sometimes used in medicines. It grows on tree trunks and stumps and can make several caps on the same tree!

The cap is hard and shaped like a horse's hoof. When it ages, it can become almost as hard as wood!

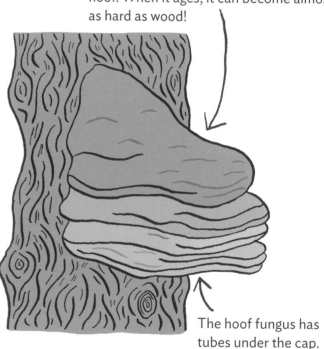

The base is attached to the wood.

The hoof fungus has tubes under the cap.

FIELD MUSHROOM

Watch out, this mushroom has some toxic lookalikes! **It grows in meadows and is also called a meadow mushroom.**

Its cap is white.

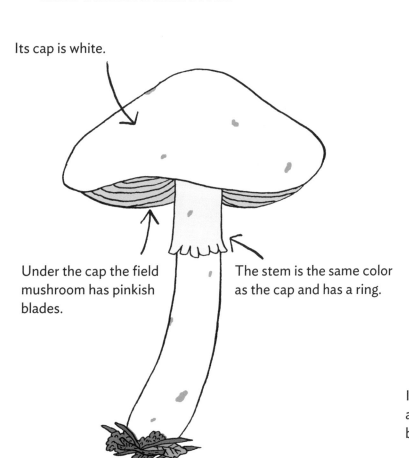

Under the cap the field mushroom has pinkish blades.

The stem is the same color as the cap and has a ring.

SHAGGY MANE

This mushroom grows in fields, in yards, and along roadsides. When it is an adult, its cap opens.

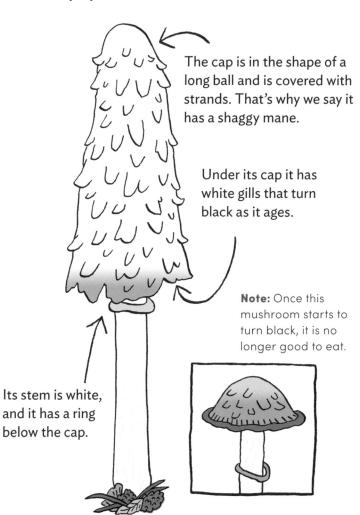

The cap is in the shape of a long ball and is covered with strands. That's why we say it has a shaggy mane.

Under its cap it has white gills that turn black as it ages.

Note: Once this mushroom starts to turn black, it is no longer good to eat.

Its stem is white, and it has a ring below the cap.

CAULIFLOWER CORAL

This mushroom grows in woods and forests. It can grow alone or in small groups forming circles called fairy rings.

Cauliflower coral is shaped like a small tree, or a piece of coral from the ocean.

The stems look like coral— or cauliflower!

The tips of the stems are often pink.

PARASOL MUSHROOM

This mushroom grows in meadows. It is also called a snake's hat or snake's sponge mushroom.

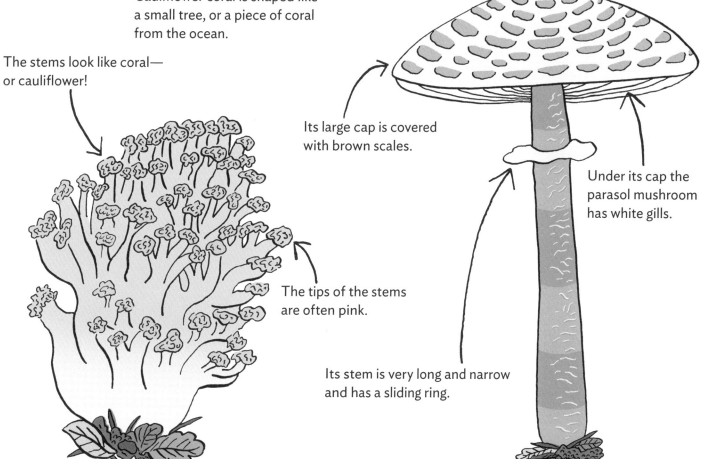

Its large cap is covered with brown scales.

Under its cap the parasol mushroom has white gills.

Its stem is very long and narrow and has a sliding ring.

HYGROSCOPIC EARTHSTAR

This mushroom grows in woods and forests. Raindrops cause its spores to come out of the center: They escape through a small hole on the top!

This funny star-shaped mushroom is made up of two parts.

The first is a ball located in the center. It is a small bag that contains the spores.

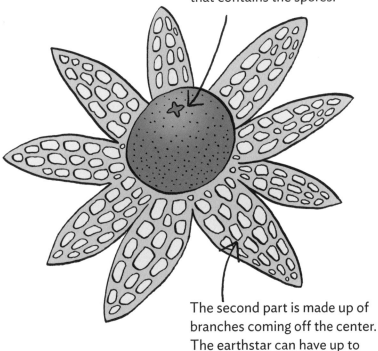

The second part is made up of branches coming off the center. The earthstar can have up to 10 branches!

DEVIL'S FINGERS

This mushroom grows in woods and forests, in yards, and around shrubs planted with mulch. In addition to having a funny shape, it also smells very bad. You can smell it from several feet away!

This bright red mushroom is shaped like a starfish!

The black spots are small, sticky bags filled with spores.